**BRITAIN:THE FACTS**

# Monarchy

Christopher Riches

**FRANKLIN WATTS**
LONDON•SYDNEY

First published in 2008
by Franklin Watts

Copyright © 2008 Christopher Riches and Trevor Bounford

Design by bounford.com

Franklin Watts
338 Euston Road
London NW1 3BH

Franklin Watts Australia
Level 17/207 Kent Street
Sydney, NSW 2000

All words in **bold** can be found in Glossary on pages 30–31. Website information is correct at time of going to press. However, the publishers cannot accept liability for any information or links found on third-party websites.

ISBN 978 0 7496 8381 8

Dewey classification: 941'.0099

Printed in China

Franklin Watts is a division of Hachette Children's Books, an Hachette Livre UK company.
www.hachettelivre.co.uk

**Picture credits**
The publishers would like to thank the following organisations for their kind permission to reproduce illustrations in this book:

Cover image © 2008 Clive Morgan/fotoLibra.
p.5 (left) © Tom Oberhofer; (top right) © 2008 Gordon Nicol/fotoLibra; (bottom right) Diagram Visual Information; p.6 (top right) © Deryc Sands (photographer), Parliamentary copyright images are reproduced with the permission of Parliament; p. 7 © World History Archive/Topfoto; p.8 (top right) Diagram Visual Information; (bottom right) © 2002 Topfoto; p. 10 (top right) © Crown copyright; (bottom right) © National Pictures/TopFoto; p. 13 (bottom right) Reproduced by kind permission of Clarence House; p. 14 © 2006 John Hedgecoe/TopFoto; p. 15 (top) © Antonio Olmos; (middle) © Martin Lubikowski; (bottom) © 2002 PA/TopFoto; p. 16 (bottom) © Jeff Moore/National Pictures/TopFoto; p. 17 (top left) © Buckingham Palace Press Office; (bottom right) © 2000 PA/TopFoto; p. 18 © bounford.com; p. 19 © bounford.com; p. 20 © Diagram Visual Information; p. 21 (top right) © Diagram Visual Information; (bottom right) The Royal Collection © 2007 Her Majesty Queen Elizabeth II; p. 22 © Diagram Visual Information; p. 23 (top left, middle left, top right) © 2004 UPP/TopFoto; (bottom right) © National Pictures/TopFoto; p. 25 © bounford.com; p. 26 (top right) © TopFoto; (bottom) © Bentley Motors; p. 27 (top right) © Print Collector/HIP/TopFoto; (bottom right) © 2004 UPP/TopFoto.

Maps and diagrams on pages 11, 12, 25 © bounford.com.

# Contents

4–5      The British Monarchy

6–7      A Constitutional Monarchy

8–9      Queen Elizabeth II

10–11    Royal Duties

12–13    The Royal Family

14–15    Some Royal Jobs

16–17    The Royal Calendar

18–19    The Royal Household

20–21    The Crown Jewels

22–23    Honours

24–25    Royal Palaces

26–27    Royal Travel

28       The Kings and Queens of Britain

29       Discussion Points, Websites

30–31    Glossary

32       Index

# The British Monarchy

The history of the British **monarchy** goes back over 1,500 years. Apart from the period called the **Commonwealth** (1649–60), monarchs (kings and queens) have always ruled. Over time power has moved from the monarchy to the Prime Minister and Parliament.

## The Kings and Queens

The right to be monarch is **inherited** (passed from parent to son or daughter). Sometimes there are no immediate **heirs** and the monarchy moves to a related family. This means that there have been different families who have ruled. Different families have also fought each other to gain the monarchy.

**1066–1154**
**The Normans** Rule established by William the Conqueror (right). He came from Normandy, in France, and conquered England after winning the battle of Hastings in 1066.

**1154–1399**
**The Plantagenets** They spread their rule and influence into France, Wales and Scotland. Named after a sprig of broom (*planta genista*) worn by the father of Henry II (right), the first Plantagenet king.

**1399–1485**
**Lancaster and York** Two different parts of the Plantagenet Royal family competed for power. The time of the War of the Roses (between Lancaster's Red Rose and York's White Rose).

**1485–1603**
**The Tudors** The Welsh Tudor family end the War of the Roses. Period dominated by two powerful monarchs – Henry VIII and Elizabeth I (right). Monarchy has great power, even changing the religion of the country.

**1603–1714**
**The Stuarts** The Stuarts were kings of Scotland who became kings of England after the death of Elizabeth. They united the two kingdoms but did not rule well. The **Civil War** led to the execution of Charles I (right) and a period of rule with no monarch (the Commonwealth (1649–60) under Oliver Cromwell).

**1714–1917**
**The Hanoverians** Replaced the Stuarts. Originally from Hanover in Germany, they left much of the detail of ruling to Parliament, whose power grew, and the Prime Minister. The monarch became more of a **figurehead**.

**1917–**
**The Windsors** The royal family renamed itself during the First World War.

## The first King of England?

It is impossible to say who was the first King of England. Alfred was King of Wessex, in southern England from 871 to 899. His kingdom was under attack from the Danes. He fought back and established his authority over many parts of England. Athelstan (924–39) extended Wessex rule over all of England and Edgar 'the Peaceful' (959–75) made England the most stable kingdom in Europe. He was followed by Aethelred 'the Unready' (978–1016), who lost it all to the Danes. William the Conqueror reunited England after the Norman conquest (1066). The coins show Aethelred (top) and William (bottom).

## What about Scotland?

The first ruler who could claim to be King of Scots was Malcolm II (1005–34). England tried to **dominate** Scotland but the army of Edward II of England was defeated at Bannockburn in 1314 by Robert the Bruce, and Scotland regained independence. The two monarchies became one, when James VI of Scotland also became James I of England in 1603 on the death of Elizabeth I.

A statue of Robert the Bruce at Bannockburn, near Stirling, where he defeated the army of Edward II of England in 1314.

## And Wales. . .

Wales never had a unified monarchy of its own. Different Royal families ruled over smaller areas. Hywel Dda (around 904–50), briefly united north and south Wales, but the unity did not last. Llyweln ap Gruffydd (1246–82) managed to reunite Wales again, only to be defeated and killed by Edward I of England, who established English rule over the whole country. He made his eldest son Prince of Wales, and the tradition of the eldest son of the English monarch being named Prince of Wales has continued.

Crown used by the Prince of Wales.

# A Constitutional Monarchy

In Britain we have a **constitutional monarchy**. This means that the monarch, currently Queen Elizabeth II, is the **Head of State**, with **ceremonial** and official duties. The country is actually run by the Prime Minister and by Parliament. This has been the case for around 300 years. Before that the monarchy had much greater power. Now the monarch has the right to be consulted and provide advice.

### Head of State and Head of Nation

The monarch has official (constitutional) duties as Head of State:

- Officially opens Parliament each year. The monarch's speech at this ceremony, written by the government, outlines its plans for the year ahead.

The Robing Room of the House of Lords, which the monarch uses before the official State Opening of Parliament in the chamber of the House of Lords.

## The English Civil War

King Charles I (1625–49) believed that a monarch only had to obey God and not the law of the country. He frequently clashed with Parliament. For 11 years he ruled without a Parliament. This led to great discontent and the start of the English Civil War between those loyal to the King and those who supported Parliament. The Parliamentarians, under Oliver Cromwell, won the war. Charles I was arrested, tried and then executed in 1649. The monarchy was abolished until 1660. It was then reintroduced, but its powers became more limited. In 1689 the Bill of Rights Act established the basis of our constitutional monarchy.

At the request of the Prime Minister, dissolves (or closes) Parliament ahead of a general election.

 Formally asks the leader of the political party with most MPs to form a government.

 Gives assent to (approves) Acts of Parliament. Assent was last refused in 1707.

 Receives (gives official status to) foreign ambassadors.

 Meets weekly with the Prime Minister.

 Entertains the Heads of State of other countries and makes overseas State Visits.

 Officially opens **Commonwealth** Heads of Government meetings.

The monarch also acts as Head of Nation:

 Is a focus for national identity.

 Provides stability (there have been 11 Prime Ministers during the Queen's reign).

 Recognises success and achievement through the **honours system**.

 Encourages public service and charitable work.

## The Abdication

After the death of George V in 1936, his eldest son, Edward, became king, as Edward VIII. However, he was never crowned because he **abdicated** (that is he gave up being king). He wished to marry Wallis Simpson. She was a **divorcee** and it was considered impossible for a monarch to marry a divorcee. He chose love and gave up his right to the throne. He had to gain approval of the Prime Minister to do this. His brother, George, became king in his place.

Times have now changed. The Prince of Wales remains first in line to succeed his mother, even though he and the Princess of Wales divorced and he remarried Camilla Parker Bowles, who was also a divorcee.

# Queen Elizabeth II

Elizabeth became Queen in 1952. She has ruled through a period of great change. The Queen is one of Britain's longest serving monarchs. Queen Victoria ruled for 63 years and George III for 59 years. She is the fortieth monarch since William the Conqueror. She married Prince Philip, Duke of Edinburgh, in 1947.

The Queen with the Duke of Edinburgh, Prince Charles and Princess Anne at Buckingham Palace after her first State Opening of Parliament in November 1952.

## Her official title

The Queen's title is 'Elizabeth the Second, by the Grace of God of the United Kingdom of Great Britain and Northern Ireland and of Her other Realms and Territories Queen, Head of the Commonwealth, Defender of the Faith'.

## The Coronation

When the Queen's father, George VI, died in 1952, she was visiting a nature reserve in Kenya. She flew home to become Queen. Her **coronation**, when she was officially crowned, took place on 2 June 1953.

## FACTS

- The Queen has given over 387,000 honours.
- She has received over 3 million letters.
- She is patron of over 620 charities.
- Her Christmas Speech was first televised in 1957.
- She has made over 250 official visits to 129 different countries.
- In 2007 a Royal Channel launched on YouTube: www.youtube.com/theroyalchannel.
- She has owned over 30 corgis (her favourite dog).
- Her wedding ring was made from a nugget of Welsh gold.
- Buckingham Palace's website was launched in 1997.
- She owns the sturgeons, whales and dolphins in British waters, based on a charter from 1324.
- When she signs official documents, she writes '*Elizabeth R*' (R stands for the Latin word *Regina*, meaning queen).

## Head of the Commonwealth

The Commonwealth is a group of countries that were once ruled by Britain or which had close connections with Britain. When the Queen came to the throne, Britain still ruled many countries (particularly in Africa). They were called **colonies**. The first colony in Africa to become independent was Ghana in 1957, and its President, Kwame Nkrumah, became the first African Head of Government in the Commonwealth. The Commonwealth now has 53 members and the Queen is the official head of the organisation.

The Commonwealth Games, open to athletes from every Commonwealth country, is held every four years. The Queen opens the Games.

The service, held in Westminster Abbey, was spectacular. The **Crown Jewels** (see page 20) played an important part .

The coronation was the first major event to be televised, at the Queen's request. Televisions at that time had very small screens and the picture was only in black-and-white. This was the first time many people had watched television.

### Golden Jubilee

In 2002, the Queen celebrated her golden jubilee. She had been Queen for 50 years. There were many celebrations. In her message to the people, she hoped: 'that this time of celebration in the United Kingdom and across the Commonwealth will not simply be an occasion to be **nostalgic** about the past. I believe that, young or old, we have as much to look forward to with confidence and hope as we have to look back on with pride.'

The Queen is Head of State of the Commonwealth countries listed below. Others have their own monarchy or elect their Head of State.

Antigua and Barbuda

Australia

The Bahamas

Barbados

Belize

Canada

Grenada

Jamaica

New Zealand

Papua New Guinea

St Christopher and Nevis

St Lucia

St Vincent and the Grenadines

Solomon Islands

Tuvalu

# Royal Duties

The Queen carries out a wide range of duties.
Every day there are jobs to be done.

### Morning
Reads a selection of daily post of 250 letters and arranges responses.
Reads, approves and signs official documents from the UK government and from around the Commonwealth.
Has official meetings (**audiences**) with **diplomats** and other individuals.

### Afternoon
Makes public visits to see people, open buildings and attend special occasions. May see government ministers.

### Evening
Once a week, on Tuesday at 6.30 p.m., she has a private meeting with the Prime Minister.
May host an official reception or banquet at Buckingham Palace.
May attend a concert or charitable event (she is the Patron of over 620 charities).

The Royal Coat of Arms. As well as being used by the monarch, it is used by the government. The French motto *Dieu et mon droit* means 'God and my right'.

The Queen and Agyekum Kufour, on his official visit as President of Ghana.

## Official visits

As Head of State the Queen entertains Heads of State when they make an official visit to this country. These are occasions of great **formality**. Recent visitors have included:

- The President of South Korea
- The President of Italy
- King Harald and Queen Sonja of Norway
- The President of the People's Republic of China
- The President of Brazil
- The President of Ghana

## What to give the Queen as a present

The Queen is given presents when she carries out official events. Some are surprising:

- Two black beavers
- A baby crocodile
- A box of snail shells
- A grove of maple trees

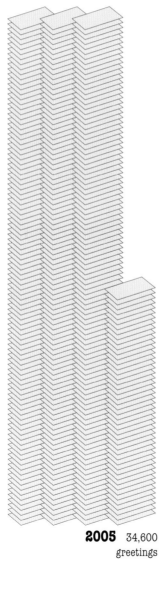

**1952**  1,390
greetings

**2005**  34,600
greetings

## Overseas trips

During her reign, the Queen has made many overseas trips (over 250 official trips). She was the first British monarch to make official visits to Russia and China. She has visited Commonwealth countries most often, making over 20 visits to Canada, 15 to Australia, 10 to New Zealand and 6 to Jamaica.

## Anniversary greetings

In 1917, George V started sending greetings to people reaching their 100th birthday. Cards are sent on the 100th and 105th birthdays and every year after that. Cards are also sent for diamond weddings (60 years), 65 years, platinum (70 years) and every year after that. Each year more greetings are sent as we live longer:

| | |
|---|---|
| 1952 | 1,390 greetings sent |
| 2005 | 34,600 greetings sent |
| 1952 | 255 people became 100 |
| 2005 | 570 people became 105 |

## FACTS

In one year the Queen

- Made 380 official appearances, including visits throughout the UK.
- Entertained 31,000 people at five **garden parties**.
- Presented honours to 2.500 people.
- Sent 34,600 anniversary messages.
- Received over 54,000 letters.

# The Royal Family

The royal family is the name given to those closely related to the monarch. The current royal family is known as the House of Windsor. The Queen's children, Charles (The Prince of Wales), Anne (The Princess Royal), Andrew (The Duke of York) and Edward (The Earl of Wessex) all carry out official duties, as do some other members of the family.

## The line of succession

1. **The Prince of Wales**

2. **Prince William of Wales**
   (son of Prince of Wales)

3. **Prince Henry of Wales**
   (son of Prince of Wales)

4. **The Duke of York**

5. **Princess Beatrice of York**
   (daughter of Duke of York)

6. **Princess Eugenie of York**
   (daughter of Duke of York)

7. **The Earl of Wessex**

8. **James, Viscount Severn**
   (son of Earl of Wessex)

9. **Lady Louise Windsor**
   (daughter of Earl of Wessex)

10. **The Princess Royal**

**GEORGE V 1910–36**
Mary of Teck d1953

**EDWARD VIII 1936 (d1972)**
Wallis Simpson (d1986)

**GEORGE VI 1936–52**
Elizabeth Bowes-Lyon (d2002)

Mary Princess Royal (d1965)

Henry, 6th Duke of Gloucester d1974
Alice Montagu-Douglas-Scott d2004

**ELIZABETH II 1952–**
Philip, Duke of Edinburgh

George, 2nd Duke of Kent d1942
Marina of Greece d1968

John d1919

⊕ Margaret d2002
Anthony Armstrong-Jones, 1st Earl of Snowdon

William d1972

Richard, 7th Duke of Gloucester
Birgitte van Deurs

Charles, Prince of Wales
⊕ Diana Spencer d1997
⊕ Camilla Parker Bowles

Anne, Princess Royal
⊕ Mark Phillips
Timothy Laurence

Andrew, Duke of York
⊕ Sarah Ferguson

Edward, Earl of Wessex
Sophie Rhys-Jones

William

Henry

Peter

Zara

David, Viscount Linley
Serena Stanhope

Sarah
Daniel Chatto

Beatrice

Eugenie

Louise

James

Charles
Margarita

Samuel
Arthur

Edward, 3rd Duke of Kent
Katherine Worsley

Alexandra
Angus Ogilvy d2004

Alexander
Claire Booth

Davina
Gary Lewis

Rose
George, Earl of St Andrews
Sylvana Tomaselli

Michael
Baroness Marie-Christine von Reibnitz

Helen
Tim Taylor

Nicholas
Paola de Frankopan

James
Julia Rawlinson

Marina
⊕ Paul Mowatt

Frederick

Gabriella

Edward
Marina
Amelia
Columbus
Cassius
Eloise
Estella

Flora
Alexander
Zenouska
Christian

⊕ = Divorced

12

## Who inherits?

The monarchy passes from one member to another within the royal family. When the monarch dies, his or her **successor** is established by the following rules:

- 👑 Sons take priority over daughters.
- 👑 Eldest son takes priority over younger sons.
- 👑 Daughters take priority over uncles.
- 👑 If a male monarch has no children, his oldest brother becomes monarch.
- 👑 If the monarch has no children and no brother, then his or her eldest sister becomes monarch.

## The Prince of Wales

Prince Charles was created the twenty-first Prince of Wales on 26 July 1958 thus becoming the first Prince of Wales since 1936. In 1969 he was '**invested**' as Prince of Wales at Caernarfon Castle, with great ceremony. In Scotland his official title is the Duke of Rothesay. His first marriage was to Lady Diana Spencer. He is now married to Camilla, Duchess of Cornwall.

## What do members of the royal family do?

Members of the royal family carry out a wide range of official functions. They assist the Queen with official duties, they make royal visits and they support many charitable and cultural organisations. In 2005, for example, the Princess Royal attended some 640 functions. She has been President of the Save the Children Fund since 1970, and works with over 200 other organisations.

## Diana, Princess of Wales

Lady Diana Spencer was brought up near Sandringham, the Queen's house in Norfolk. In 1981, aged 20, she married the Prince of Wales in a glittering wedding service at St Paul's Cathedral. Around the world 1,000 million people watched on television or listened on the radio. She brought glamour to the royal family and a popular touch. By meeting with AIDS victims, she removed some of the prejudice against them. The marriage ended in divorce in 1996, and she died following a car crash in Paris in 1997. She was referred to as the 'People's Princess'.

The badge of The Prince of Wales was first used by Edward the Black Prince (1330–76), the eldest son of Edward III. *Ich Dien* is German for 'I serve'.

# Some Royal Jobs

The monarch holds many particular official positions. There are also many official appointments made by the monarch.

## Head of the Armed Forces

The monarch is Head of the Armed Forces. If the country goes to war, it is in the name of the monarch. The decision, however, is taken by the Prime Minister and Parliament. The monarch is Colonel-in-Chief of many army regiments in Britain and in Commonwealth countries.

## Head of the Church of England

The monarch is Supreme Governor of the Church of England. The title goes back to Henry VIII. He broke away from the Roman Catholic Church in the **Reformation** and ensured that the monarch was head of the Church. The monarch appoints all the **bishops** of the Church, now on the advice of the Prime Minister. The Church of England is called an 'established' Church, because the State plays a part in its life.

## Church of Scotland

The Church of Scotland is the established Church in Scotland. The monarch takes an oath to preserve the Church of Scotland. However, the monarch is just a member of the Church rather than a 'supreme governor'. The monarch is represented at the annual General Assembly, the ruling body of the Church.

The Queen, riding side saddle, at the Trooping of the Colour (see page 16).

Some of the other positions the monarch holds are:

- Head of the Privy Council
- The Fount of Justice
- In the Isle of Man, Lord of Man
- In the Channel Islands, Lord of Normandy

# Special Royal appointments

The monarch makes a number of special appointments.

### The Poet Laureate

Charles II appointed John Dryden as the first Poet Laureate in 1668. The Poet Laureate was expected to write poems to celebrate royal events. Famous poets who have held the post include William Wordsworth, Alfred Tennyson, John Betjeman and Ted Hughes. The current laureate is Andrew Motion. The post is so called after the wreath of laurel leaves that the ancient Greeks crowned their poets with. Originally payment included a cask of canary (a type of wine). It has now been replaced by a cask of sherry.

### The Astronomer Royal

The Royal Observatory at Greenwich.

Charles II appointed John Flamsteed as the first Astronomer Royal in 1675 to help improve astronomical tables used in **navigation**. At the same time he established the world-famous Royal Observatory in Greenwich Park (right). The current Astronomer Royal is Professor Martin Rees.

### The Master of the Queen's Music

From medieval times, royal courts had bands of musicians to entertain the monarch. Charles I was the first King to appoint a 'Master of the King's Music' in 1626. Peter Maxwell Davies is the current Master, and writes music for royal celebrations.

### The Queen's Piper

The Queen's Piper.

The Queen's Piper (right) is a serving soldier. His main task is to play the bagpipes at 9 a.m. every weekday for about 15 minutes under the Queen's window when she is at Buckingham Palace, Windsor Castle, the Palace of Holyroodhouse or Balmoral Castle. Pipers also play at State banquets.

# The Royal Calendar

There are ceremonies that the Queen undertakes every year. They form part of the ceremonial life of Britain.

### January

New Year's Honours (now
   announced 31 December)
Epiphany Service, Chapel Royal,
   St James' Palace

### February

Accession Day (6 February)

### March/April

Royal Maundy Service (the Thursday before Easter)

### April

Queen's Birthday (21 April)

### June

Coronation Day (2 June)
Duke of Edinburgh's
   Birthday (10 June)
Queen's Official Birthday
   (first or second Saturday)
Queen's Birthday Honours
Trooping of the Colour
Royal Ascot Races
Garter Day at Windsor Castle

## Maundy Service

On Maundy Thursday (the Thursday before Easter), the monarch gives Maundy money to pensioners. This tradition is over 700 years old. It also used to involve the monarch washing the feet of the pensioners, commemorating Jesus' act of washing his **disciples**' feet at the **Last Supper**. The service is held each year in a different cathedral in England. The number of pensioners is linked to the monarch's age. If the monarch is 70, then 70 men and 70 women each receive 70p in special Maundy money. The coins are made of silver and are specially made for the occasion.

## Trooping of the Colour

This military ceremony involves soldiers from the **Foot Guards** and the **Household Cavalry**. Their ceremonial duties include providing the guard at Buckingham Palace. It takes place on Horse Guards Parade in Whitehall, in central London, on the monarch's official birthday. It has happened since 1748.

Its original purpose was to carry (troop) the flags (colours) through all the ranks of the soldiers so that they would recognise the flags in battle.

## Garden Parties

In the summer the Queen holds garden parties at Buckingham Palace and Holyroodhouse. Around 8,000 people are invited to each party. They will get through:

- 27,000 cups of tea
- 20,000 sandwiches
- 20,000 slices of cake

### July

Garden Party, Holyroodhouse

Swan Upping

Garden Parties, Buckingham Palace

### September

Braemar Highland Games

### November

State Opening of Parliament

Remembrance Day

Prince of Wales' Birthday
    (14 November)

Royal Variety
    Performance

### December

Queen's Christmas
    Broadcast

## Swan Upping

The monarch shares ownership of the swans on the River Thames with the Vintners' and Dyers' companies (historic bodies that used to control the wine and clothes dyeing trades respectively). In July each year the Queen's Swan Marker and the Swan Uppers of the Vintners and Dyers spend five days in rowing boats going up a stretch of the Thames recording all the swans they see. In 2005, 88 young swans were recorded. The ceremony started in the twelfth century, when swans used to be eaten as a great delicacy at royal banquets.

# The Royal Household

The Royal Household supports the Queen in carrying out her official duties. The head of the Royal Household is called the Lord Chamberlain. Other key officials are:

**BY APPOINTMENT TO HER MAJESTY THE QUEEN**

### The Private Secretary

- Deals with governments, armed forces, churches and other organisations.
- Organises the monarch's official programme.

### The Keeper of the Privy Purse

- Manages all the financial affairs of the monarch.
- Looks after the maintenance of the royal palaces.

### The Master of the Household

- Organises all the catering and official entertaining.
- Looks after all the housekeeping.

### The Comptroller of the Lord Chamberlain's Office

- Organises all ceremonial events.
- Arranges honours and Royal Warrants.

## Royal Warrants

The Queen, the Duke of Edinburgh and the Prince of Wales give '**warrants**' to particular businesses that provide them with goods or services. Each business can then use the Royal Crest and the words 'By Appointment'. Among the goods supplied by warrant holders are:

Besom brooms and pea sticks

Chimney sweeps

Chocolates

Christmas crackers

Executive toilet hire

Goldleaf

Marmalade

Mole controllers

Ready mixed concrete

Robes

## The Queen's wealth

Most of the wealth of the monarch is linked to the position of Head of State. The Queen cannot sell the Crown Jewels, paintings from the Royal Collection or land in the Crown Estate for her own profit. Her personal wealth comes from owning the Sandringham and Balmoral estates and a wide range of investments. The total value may be around £250 million – very different from the value of the Crown Estate, alone valued at over £7 billion.

## What do they do?

**Lady in Waiting:** Accompanies the Queen on official visits (and helps to carry cards and presents on walkabouts); also helps with the Queen's correspondence, particularly to children.

**Queen's Equerry:** A military officer who accompanies the Queen at official occasions and is involved in the detailed planning of the Queen's programme.

**Crown Equerry:** In charge of the Royal Mews (see page 26).

**Page of the Presence:** Looks after the Queen's guests.

**Page of Honour:** Carries the train of the Queen's Robe of State.

**Footmen:** Royal servants; their day uniform is a black tail coat and trousers, white shirt with black tie and scarlet waistcoat; on special occasions, scarlet **livery** decorated with gold braid, scarlet plush knee breeches, pink stockings and black buckle shoes.

## Royal finances

The monarch receives money from the government. In 2006 this amounted to 62p for everyone in the country, a total of around £37 million. The main expenditure included:

- The Civil List (to cover the costs of the official duties of the monarch).
- Looking after the royal palaces.
- Travelling costs for official visits.
- The Privy Purse for the monarch's public and personal use.

The Prince of Wales pays for his own costs from income he receives from the Duchy of Cornwall. The estate of the Duchy was created in 1337 by Edward III specifically to provide an income to the Prince of Wales. It now owns around 55,000 hectares of land in the south west of England.

The Duchy of Cornwall produces a range of organic food, a keen interest of the Prince of Wales.

The Queen pays other members of the royal family out of income from the Duchy of Lancaster. The origin of the Duchy dates from 1265 and it became part of the royal estates in 1399. It owns property in London and around 19,000 hectares of land in northern England.

# The Crown Jewels

The first Crown Jewels were probably made for Edward the Confessor (1042–66). The most important of the Crown Jewels are those used in the coronation (the 'crowning') of the monarch. Each item has a particular **symbolism**. Together they are called the Royal **Regalia**. Most date from the time of Charles II (1660–85).

## The Royal Regalia used at the Coronation

- Three swords: symbols of mercy and justice.
- The Great **Seal** of State: the symbol of royal authority.
- St Edward's staff: to guide the monarch's footsteps.
- The ampulla and spoon: the ampulla, an eagle-shaped flask, holds holy oil that the **Archbishop of Canterbury** uses to anoint the monarch. The spoon is the oldest item, probably made for Henry II.
- **Spurs**: symbols of knighthood and chivalry.
- Armills (gold bracelets): symbols of wisdom and sincerity.
- The Orb: a globe with a cross at the top, symbolising Christian rule of the world.
- The coronation ring: symbol of the dignity of the monarchy.
- The Sceptre with the Cross: symbol of earthly power.

# FACTS

- The Imperial State Crown contains 2,268 diamonds, 17 sapphires, 11 emeralds, 5 rubies and 273 pearls.

- It contains a sapphire from Edward the Confessor's ring, pearls from Elizabeth I and a ruby given by Pedro the Cruel to Edward the Black Prince in 1367.

- The Sceptre with the Cross holds one of the largest cut diamonds in the world, the Cullinan I diamond, the 'Star of Africa'.

- The crown made for Queen Elizabeth, the Queen Mother for the coronation in 1937 contains the diamond called the Koh-i-noor (the Mountain of Light). Known from 1300 in India, it was given to Queen Victoria in 1850 following the conquest of the Punjab.

The Orb (above) is made of over 1 kilogram of gold and contains more than 600 jewels and pearls. The Sceptre with dove (right) is a gold rod over 1 metre in length. The dove is a symbol of God.

The Crown Jewels are very important to the monarchy, but they have had troubled times:

- In 1216 King John lost his Crown Jewels when they were being taken across the Wash in eastern England. They have never been found.
- In 1289 Edward III raised money with them to pay his troops.
- In 1649 Oliver Cromwell sold the jewels and melted down the metal after the English Civil War.
- In 1671 Captain Blood tried to steal them. He was caught leaving the Tower of London with a crown, a sceptre and the orb.

- The Sceptre with dove (sometimes called the Rod of Equity and Mercy): symbol of the spiritual role of the monarchy.
- St Edward's Crown: symbol of monarchy. The crown was made for Charles II, following the style of Edward the Confessor's crown.

St Edward's Crown is used to crown the monarch in the coronation service.

## The Coronation Chair

This was made around 1300 for Edward I. It has been used for nearly every coronation since that of Edward II in 1308. It is one of the oldest pieces of wooden furniture in Britain. It was especially designed to include the **Stone of Destiny**, used in the coronation of the Scottish kings and taken in 1296 by Edward I from Scone. The stone was returned to Scotland in 1996.

## The Honours of Scotland

The oldest British Crown Jewels are those of Scotland, called the Honours of Scotland. They can be seen at Edinburgh Castle. The crown, of Scottish gold, was made in 1540; the sceptre, given by Pope Alexander VI, was made in 1494 and the Sword of State was presented in 1507 by Pope Julius II. They were last used in the coronation of Charles II at Scone in 1651.

The Honours of Scotland is the name for the Scottish Crown Jewels.

# Honours

The monarch has always rewarded individuals for their **loyalty** and for personal achievements. Sometimes a monarch would give land. More often he would give a title, medal or some other mark that would be recognised. For the monarch these honours had the advantage of reinforcing people's loyalty while not costing the monarchy money. Out of this has developed the honours system we have today. Some honours are made directly by the monarch. Others are made on the recommendation of the Prime Minister.

## Why the Garter?

For such a noble order, the **garter** seems a strange choice of name. One story suggests that at a ball, the Countess of Salisbury, to her great embarrassment, dropped one of her garters, while dancing with King Edward III. He picked it up and put it round his own leg saying, 'Honi soit qui mal y pense', which became the motto of the Order. There seems to be no truth in this. The garter is thought to refer to a strap used to fasten pieces of armour, and the motto refers to the people who opposed the King's plans to conquer France.

## The Order of the Garter

Founded in 1348 by King Edward III as a military **order** to strengthen his campaign against the French. There are 24 Knights of the Garter.

**Motto:** *Honi soit qui mal y pense* (Shame on him who evil thinks).

## The Order of the Thistle

A Scottish Order, said by some to have been founded in the ninth century, but actually established in its current form in 1687 by King James VII of Scotland (James II of England). There are 16 Knights of the Thistle.

**Motto:** *Nemo me impune lacessit* (no one attacks me unpunished).

### The Order of Merit

Founded in 1902 to honour achievement in arts, learning, literature and science. There are 24 members.

**Motto:** For merit.

### Companion of Honour

Founded in 1917 to honour service of national importance. There are 65 members.

**Motto:** In action faithful and in honour clear.

### The Order of the Bath

Founded in 1725 and named after the ritual washing of a person before becoming a **knight**. Now used to honour military officers. There are 1,860 members in three ranks.

**Motto:** *Tria juncta in uno* (three joined in one).

## New Year and Birthday Honours

Twice a year, at New Year and on the Queen's official birthday in June, honours are given to around 1,000 people for service to their community and country. The highest award is a knighthood (allowing the person to be called 'Sir'). Most awards are within the Order of the British Empire – Member (MBE), Officer (OBE), Commander (CBE), Knight or Dame (KBE, DBE). There are over 100,000 living members of the Order. The Queen or a member of the royal family presents the honours at an **investiture**, usually at Buckingham Palace. There are around 20 each year.

# Royal Palaces

The royal palaces are where the monarch carries out the official duties as Head of State. Monarchs have always used palaces as a way of showing their authority. The royal flag flies when the monarch is staying there. The costs of palaces are met by the government. Balmoral and Sandringham are the Queen's private houses.

### Royal palaces

1. Buckingham Palace, London
2. St James's Palace, London
3. Clarence House, London
4. Kensington Palace, London
5. Windsor Castle, Windsor
6. Holyroodhouse, Edinburgh

### Royal palaces and houses no longer used by the monarch

7. Hampton Court Palace, London
8. Tower of London, London
9. Osborne House, Isle of Wight
10. Royal Pavilion, Brighton
11. Banqueting House, Whitehall
12. The Queen's House, Greenwich

### Queen's private houses

13. Balmoral, Scottish Highlands
14. Sandringham, Norfolk

## Buckingham Palace

Buckingham Palace was originally the London home of the Duke of Buckingham. It was bought by George III in 1761 as a family home. The first monarch to use it as the official London palace was Queen Victoria. All following monarchs have stayed there. The original house has been enlarged many times. The East Front (the most familiar view) was completed in 1914. The palace is used for many formal occasions.

BUCKINGHAM PALACE, LONDON.

24

## Windsor Castle

William the Conqueror started to build the castle in the 1070s, and it has been a royal castle ever since. It is the largest occupied castle in the world. Many monarchs have added buildings. Edward III built St George's Hall for the Knights of the Garter, and Edward IV built St George's Chapel, where ten monarchs are buried. In 1992 there was a serious fire, and many rooms were damaged. They have now all been restored.

East Terrace, Windsor Castle.

9

## Palace of Holyroodhouse

This is the royal palace in Edinburgh. Originally an abbey founded by King David I in 1128, the first palace building dates from 1501. Its most famous resident was Mary, Queen of Scots. It was enlarged by Charles II, but he never lived there. It was used by Bonnie Prince Charlie in 1745 in the **Jacobite** rising, when he tried to claim the British throne.

In 1566, Holyroodhouse witnessed a violent murder. Mary, Queen of Scots, pregnant with the future James VI, was playing cards with her private secretary, David Rizzio. A gang of Scottish nobles, led by her husband, Lord Darnley, burst in and dragged Rizzio from her side, stabbing him over 50 times. It is said that his blood still stains the floor of the room. In 1568 Mary fled to England, only to be held captive by her cousin, Elizabeth I. She was beheaded in 1587.

## Balmoral and Sandringham

Balmoral, in the Highlands of Scotland, and Sandringham, in Norfolk (below), are both owned privately by the Queen. She spends the late summer at Balmoral, originally built for Queen Victoria and Prince Albert in 1856. From Christmas to February she stays at Sandringham, purchased in 1862 by Queen Victoria as a house for her son, the future Edward VII. The house was rebuilt in 1870.

# Royal Travel

The Queen may travel in anything from a horse-drawn **carriage** to an aeroplane. The royal cars even include an LPG-powered London taxi, used by the Duke of Edinburgh.

## The carriages

The Queen has a collection of over 100 carriages, kept in the Royal Mews at Buckingham Palace. Mews is an old word for stables. There are around 30 carriage horses kept at the Mews, mostly Cleveland Greys. The newest coach is the State Coach Britannia, a gift in 2008 from Australia for the Queen's 80th birthday. It has electric windows, heating and **hydraulic suspension**!

The Queen in an open carriage.

## Royal cars

The Queen has eight **limousines** for use on official occasions.

The newest were given to the Queen in 2002. Specially designed, they have a very light rear cabin, but, at the request of the Queen, few electronic gadgets. They can use LPG fuel as well as petrol and have a maximum speed of 120 m.p.h.

The newest Royal limousine. It is a Bentley and only two were ever made.

The State limousines are the only cars in the UK that do not have number plates. As a result they are not eligible to pay congestion charges in London.

## The Gold State Coach

The oldest carriage is the Gold State Coach. It was built for George III and was first used in 1762.

- ♛ It weighs 4 tonnes.
- ♛ It needs 8 horses to pull it.
- ♛ It is 3.6 m high and 7 m long.
- ♛ It is covered in gold leaf.
- ♛ The decoration includes 4 lions, 1 crown, 8 palm trees and 4 tritons (half man, half fish).
- ♛ Painted panels celebrate Britain's military successes.

For all its magnificence, it was very uncomfortable. Travelling in it was like being in a ship tossed in a storm, according to William IV.

## Royal train

The Queen makes longer journeys by train. There are eight special royal coaches which are painted maroon with a grey roof. The Queen's coach contains a bedroom, a bathroom and a sitting room. The first royal train journey, in 1842, lasted 25 minutes, when Queen Victoria went from Slough to London.

## Royal aircraft

The Royal Household has one helicopter that is used for many short official trips. The Queen also uses two aeroplanes operated by the Ministry of Defence.

## HM Yacht Britannia

For nearly 44 years *Britannia* travelled round the world on official visits. In 1997 it went out of service and can now be visited at the Ocean Terminal at Leith, near Edinburgh. It travelled over 1 million miles and made 696 overseas visits and 272 home visits. One tradition was that no shouted orders were ever given – hand signals and written orders kept things quiet on board.

# The Kings and Queens of Britain

The lists below give the monarchs of England, Scotland and the United Kingdom. The dates show when each monarch ruled.

## Early English kings

| | |
|---|---|
| Alfred the Great | 871–99 |
| Edward the Elder | 899–924 |
| Athelstan | 924–39 |
| Edmund I | 939–46 |
| Edred | 946–55 |
| Edwy | 955–59 |
| Edgar the Peaceful | 959–75 |
| Edward the Martyr | 975–78 |
| Aethelred II the Unready | 978–1016 |
| Canute (Cnut) | 1016–35 |
| Harold I | 1035–40 |
| Hardicanute (Harhacnut) | 1040–42 |
| Edward the Confessor | 1042–66 |
| Harold II | 1066 |

## Kings and queens of England (from 1603, Kings of Britain)

### The Normans

| | |
|---|---|
| William I | 1066–87 |
| William II | 1087–1100 |
| Henry I | 1100–35 |
| Stephen | 1135–54 |

### The Plantagenets

| | |
|---|---|
| Henry II | 1154–89 |
| Richard I | 1189–99 |
| John | 1199–1216 |
| Henry III | 1216–72 |
| Edward I | 1272–1307 |
| Edward II | 1307–27 |
| Edward III | 1327–77 |
| Richard II | 1377–99 |

### Lancaster and York

| | |
|---|---|
| Henry IV | 1399–1413 |
| Henry V | 1413–22 |
| Henry VI | 1422–61, 1470–71 |
| Edward IV | 1461–70, 1471–83 |
| Edward V | 1483 |
| Richard III | 1483–85 |

### The Tudors

| | |
|---|---|
| Henry VII | 1485–1509 |
| Henry VIII | 1509–47 |
| Edward VI | 1547–53 |
| Mary I | 1553–58 |
| Elizabeth I | 1558–1603 |

### The Stuarts

| | |
|---|---|
| James I | 1603–25 |
| Charles I | 1625–49 |
| Charles II | 1660–85 |
| James II | 1685–88 |
| William III | 1689–1702 |
| *jointly with* Mary II | 1689–94 |
| Anne | 1702–14 |

### The Hanoverians

| | |
|---|---|
| George I | 1714–27 |
| George II | 1727–60 |
| George III | 1760–1820 |
| George IV | 1820–30 |
| William IV | 1830–37 |
| Victoria | 1837–1901 |
| Edward VII | 1901–10 |

### The Windsors

(George V changed the name to the House of Windsor in 1917)

| | |
|---|---|
| George V | 1910–36 |
| Edward VIII | 1936 |
| George VI | 1936–52 |
| Elizabeth II | 1952– |

## Scotland

The crowns of England and Scotland were united under James I (James VI of Scotland) in 1603. Before that there were separate monarchies.

| | |
|---|---|
| Malcolm II | 1005–34 |
| Duncan I | 1034–40 |
| Macbeth | 1040–57 |
| Luluch | 1057–58 |
| Malcolm III Canmore | 1058–93 |
| Donald III Ban | 1093–94, 1094–97 |
| Duncan II | 1094 |
| Edgar | 1097–1107 |
| Alexander I | 1107–24 |
| David I | 1124–53 |
| Malcolm IV | 1153–65 |
| William I the Lion | 1165–1214 |
| Alexander II | 1214–49 |
| Alexander III | 1249–86 |
| Margaret | 1286–90 |
| John Balliol | 1292–96 |
| Robert the Bruce | 1306–29 |
| David II | 1329–33, 1336–71 |
| Edward Balliol | 1332, 1333–34, 1335–36 |
| Robert II | 1371–90 |
| Robert III | 1390–1406 |
| James I | 1406–37 |
| James II | 1437–60 |
| James III | 1460–88 |
| James IV | 1488–1513 |
| James V | 1513–42 |
| Mary, Queen of Scots | 1542–67 |
| James VI | 1567–1625 |

# Discussion Points

- The monarch is the Head of State. What do you think is the most important task of the monarch? (**pages 6–7**)

- Suggest reasons why it is good that the Head of State is not a political figure and serves for a long time? (**pages 6–7**)

- The role of monarch is inherited. What are the strengths and weaknesses of this system?

- Find out about other countries where the Queen is Head of State. (**page 9**)

- Why do you think that the Queen is now sending out more anniversary messages than in 1952? (**page 11**)

- The Crown Jewels symbolise various virtues. Which do you think are most important in a leader? (**pages 20–21**)

- What features would you add to a new royal carriage? (**page 26**)

- What would you do if you were the monarch?

# Websites

There are many sites on the Internet about Britain's monarchy.

The official royal website is the place to start: **www.royal.gov.uk**. The main sections cover the monarchy today; the royal family; the history of the British monarchy; the palaces. There is much more within the site that is not quite so easy to find. Here are two suggestions:
Kid's zone:
**www.royal.gov.uk/output/ page218.asp** and
Fact Files:
**www.royal.gov.uk/output/page3953.asp**

To find out more about the royal palaces (including information on visiting), go to **www.royalcollection.org.uk**

To find out more about the HM Yacht *Britannia*, go to **www.royalyachtbritannia.co.uk**

To see a selection of royal videos, go to **www.youtube.com/theroyalchannel**

The Prince of Wales has his own website **www.princeofwales.gov.uk** that provides lots of information on the Prince, his family and the many activities he is involved with. See also the Duchy of Cornwall site **www.duchyofcornwall.org.uk**

**Note to parents and teachers:** Every effort has been made by the Publishers to ensure that these websites are suitable for children, that they are of the highest educational value, and that they contain no inappropriate or offensive material. However, because of the nature of the Internet, it is impossible to guarantee that the contents of these sites will not be altered. We strongly advise that Internet access is supervised by a responsible adult.

# Glossary

**abdicate** To stop ruling as a monarch. Normally a monarch rules until he or she dies. Only in special circumstances is a monarch able to abdicate.

**Archbishop of Canterbury** The leader of the Church of England and the worldwide Anglican church.

**audience** A formal meeting with the monarch.

**bishop** A church leader. A bishop leads the church in an area (a diocese) of the country.

**cathedral** A large church that is used by the bishop of the surrounding area.

**ceremonial** Describing the formal events undertaken by a monarch, such as the State Opening of Parliament.

**civil war** A war between different groups within a country rather than a war between countries.

**colonies** Countries that were under the control of a distant foreign country.

**Commonwealth** 1. The period between 1649 and 1660, following the English Civil War, when there was no monarch.
2. The organisation of countries that used to be ruled directly by Britain.

**constitutional monarchy** A country where the monarch is Head of State but where the government is controlled by an elected parliament.

**coronation** The ceremony at which a king or queen is crowned and becomes monarch of the country.

**Crown Jewels** The monarch's official jewels, including the crown, orb and sceptre. They are used in the coronation ceremony.

**diplomat** An official representative of one country in another.

**disciple** A follower of a teacher or leader. The disciples of Jesus were his 12 closest supporters.

**divorcee** Someone who has been divorced after a couple's marriage has failed.

**dominate** To have the most power in a particular situation.

**figurehead** Someone seen as the leader of a particular group. Originally it was the name of the carved head at the front of a ship.

**Foot Guards** Five regiments (Grenadier, Coldstream, Scots, Irish and Welsh Guards) in the Household Division who carry out their duties on foot. They wear bright red uniforms and tall bearskin caps.

**formality** Behaviour that follows strict rules rather than being relaxed or casual.

**garden party** A formal party held outside in a private garden, usually during the afternoon.

**garter** A piece of fabric at the top of a stocking or sock that is used to hold it up.

**gold leaf** a very thin sheet of gold that is used to decorate things

**Head of State** The individual who is the formal leader of the country. In many countries, including Britain, the Head of State is a ceremonial position.

**heir** A person who will inherit a title or property from a relative. The heir to the throne is next in line to become monarch.

**honours system** The system that honours individuals who have made notable contributions to their local community or to the country.

**Household Cavalry** Two regiments (Life Guards and the Blues and Royals) in the Household Division who carry out most of their duties on horseback.

**hydraulic suspension** A mechanism that gives a smooth ride to a vehicle. Rather than using springs of metal, the springing is provided by liquid under pressure.

**inherit** To receive something from somebody who has died; it can include a noble title.

**investiture** An occasion when honours or a title are awarded (**invested**).

**Jacobite** A Scottish supporter of the Stuart kings after the Hanoverians took the British crown. Bonnie Prince Charlie led the Jacobites in the 1745 Rising.

**knight** Originally a military supporter of the monarch, but now an honorary title given to a person in recognition of a major contribution to the life of the country.

**Last Supper** The last meal that Jesus had with his disciples before he was betrayed, arrested and executed. At the meal Jesus washed the feet of his disciples.

**limousine** A large and luxurious car used by the monarch on official occasions.

**livery** The name for an official uniform worn by a servant of the monarch.

**loyalty** The showing of clear support and duty to someone else.

**Monarch** A king or queen who is the Head of State of a country.

**navigation** The plotting of a safe course from one place to another.

**nostalgic** Describing a feeling of pleasure when remembering events in the past.

**order** The name given to a particular type of honour, originally used to describe a group of knights who worked together for the monarch.

**Reformation** A period in the sixteenth century when some Christians split from the Roman Catholic church to form a number of Protestant churches.

**regalia** Ceremonial objects and clothes used at the coronation of the monarch.

**seal** A mark on an official document to show that it is genuine.

**spurs** Metal spikes attached to a horse-rider's boots. They can be pressed into the horse to make it go faster.

**Stone of Destiny** A block of stone, used in the coronation ceremony of Scottish kings for over 1,000 years. In 1296 Edward I took it from Scotland to London. It was returned to Scotland in 1996.

**successor** A person who takes over a position from its previous holder.

**symbolism** The use of objects to represent ideas, for example the Royal Regalia symbolise aspects of the Monarch's power.

**warrant** An official document that gives its holder particular rights.

# Index

abdication, 7

armed forces, 14

Astronomer Royal, 15

Balmoral, 24, 25

Bath, Order of, 23

birthday messages, 11

*Britannia*, HM Yacht, 27

British Empire, Order of, 23

Buckingham Palace, 24

Church of England, 14

Church of Scotland, 14

Civil List, 19

Civil War, English, 6

Coat of Arms, Royal, 10

Commonwealth (of Nations), 9

Commonwealth (1649–60), 4

Comptroller, 18

coronation, 8, 9, 20

Coronation Chair, 21

Crown Jewels, 20, 21

Diana, Princess of Wales, 13

Duchy of Cornwall, 19

Duchy of Lancaster, 19

Edinburgh, Duke of, 8

Edward VIII, 7

Elizabeth II, 6, 8, 9

equerry, 19

family tree, 12

footmen, 19

garden party, 17

Garter, Order of, 22

Gold State Coach, 27

golden jubilee, 9

Hanoverians, 4

Head of State, 6, 7

Holyroodhouse, 25

Honour, Companion of, 23

honours system, 22, 23

inheritance, 4, 13

investiture, 23

Keeper of the Privy Purse, 18

kings and queens, list of, 28

lady in waiting, 19

Lancaster and York, 4

Lord Chamberlain, 18

Master of the Household, 18

Master of the Queen's Music, 15

Maundy service, 16

Merit, Order of, 23

monarchy, constitutional, 6, 7

Normans, 4

official visits, 10

overseas trips, 11

Plantagenets, 4

Poet Laureate, 15

presents, for Queen, 11

Private Secretary, 18

Queen, wealth of, 18, 19

Queen's Piper, 15

royal aircraft, 27

royal cars, 26

royal ceremonies, 16, 17

royal family, 12, 13

Royal Household, 18, 19

Royal Mews, 26

royal palaces, 24, 25

royal train, 27

Royal Warrant, 18

Sandringham, 24, 25

Scotland, Honours of, 21

Scotland, monarchs of, 5, 28

Stone of Destiny, 21

Stuarts, 4

succession, line of, 12

Swan Upping, 17

Thistle, Order of, 22

Trooping of the Colour, 16

Tudors, 4

Wales, rulers of, 5

Wales, Prince of, 5, 7, 13, 19

Windsor Castle, 24

Windsors, 4